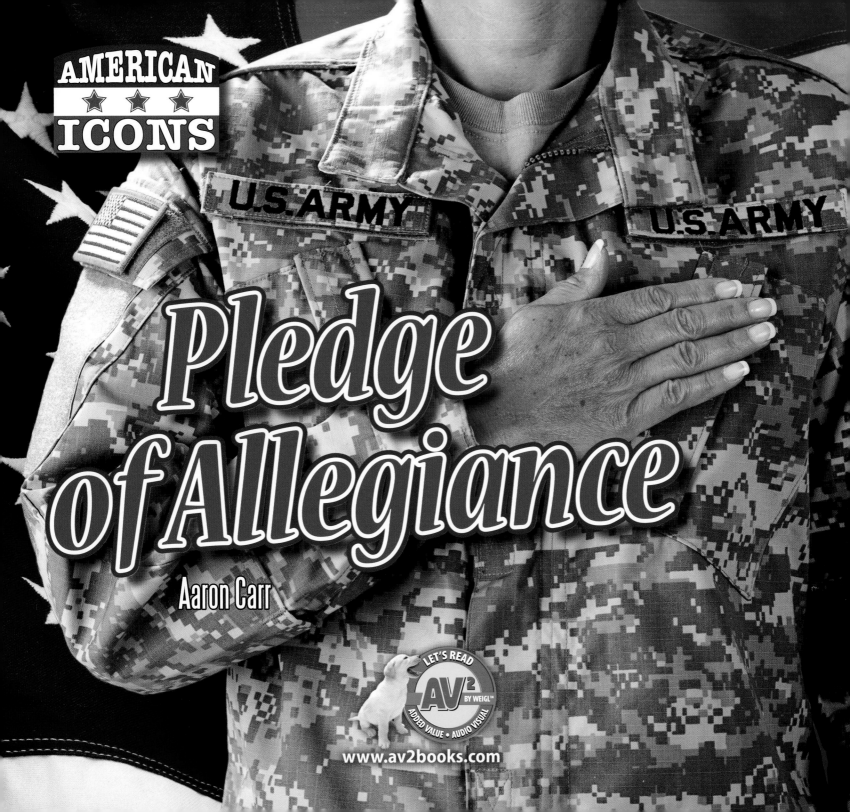

AMERICAN ICONS

★ ★ ★

Pledge of Allegiance

Aaron Carr

LET'S READ
AV2 BY WEIGL™
ADDED VALUE • AUDIO VISUAL

www.av2books.com

LET'S READ
AV²
BY WEIGL™
ADDED VALUE • AUDIO VISUAL

Go to **www.av2books.com**, and enter this book's unique code.

BOOK CODE

F397997

AV² by Weigl brings you media enhanced books that support active learning.

AV² provides enriched content that supplements and complements this book. Weigl's AV² books strive to create inspired learning and engage young minds in a total learning experience.

Your AV² Media Enhanced books come alive with...

Audio
Listen to sections of the book read aloud.

Key Words
Study vocabulary, and complete a matching word activity.

Video
Watch informative video clips.

Quizzes
Test your knowledge.

Embedded Weblinks
Gain additional information for research.

Slide Show
View images and captions, and prepare a presentation.

Try This!
Complete activities and hands-on experiments.

... and much, much more!

Published by AV² by Weigl
350 5th Avenue, 59th Floor New York, NY   10118
Websites: www.av2books.com   www.weigl.com

Library of Congress Cataloging-in-Publication Data
Carr, Aaron.
 Pledge of Allegiance / Aaron Carr.
     pages cm. -- (American icons)
  ISBN 978-1-4896-2902-9 (hardcover : alk. paper) -- ISBN 978-1-4896-2903-6 (softcover : alk. paper) -- ISBN 978-1-4896-2904-3 (single-user ebk.) -- ISBN 978-1-4896-2905-0 (multi-user ebk.)
 1. Bellamy, Francis. Pledge of Allegiance to the Flag--Juvenile literature. 2. Flags--United States--Juvenile literature. I. Title.
  JC346.C39 2015
  323.6'50973--dc23
                              2014038566

Printed in the United States of America in North Mankato, Minnesota
1 2 3 4 5 6 7 8 9 0   18 17 16 15 14

122014
WEP311214

Project Coordinator: Heather Kissock
Designer: Mandy Christiansen

Every reasonable effort has been made to trace ownership and to obtain permission to reprint copyright material. The publishers would be pleased to have any errors or omissions brought to their attention so that they may be corrected in subsequent printings.

Weigl acknowledges Getty Images and iStock as the primary image suppliers for this title.

CONTENTS

What Is the Pledge of Allegiance?

The Pledge of Allegiance is a promise to be true to the flag of the United States. Americans say the pledge to show that they love their country.

I pledge allegiance to the flag
of the United States of America
and to the Republic
for which it stands,
one nation under God, indivisible,
with liberty and justice for all.

A National Symbol

The Pledge of Allegiance was written after the Civil War came to an end. The pledge became a symbol of a united country.

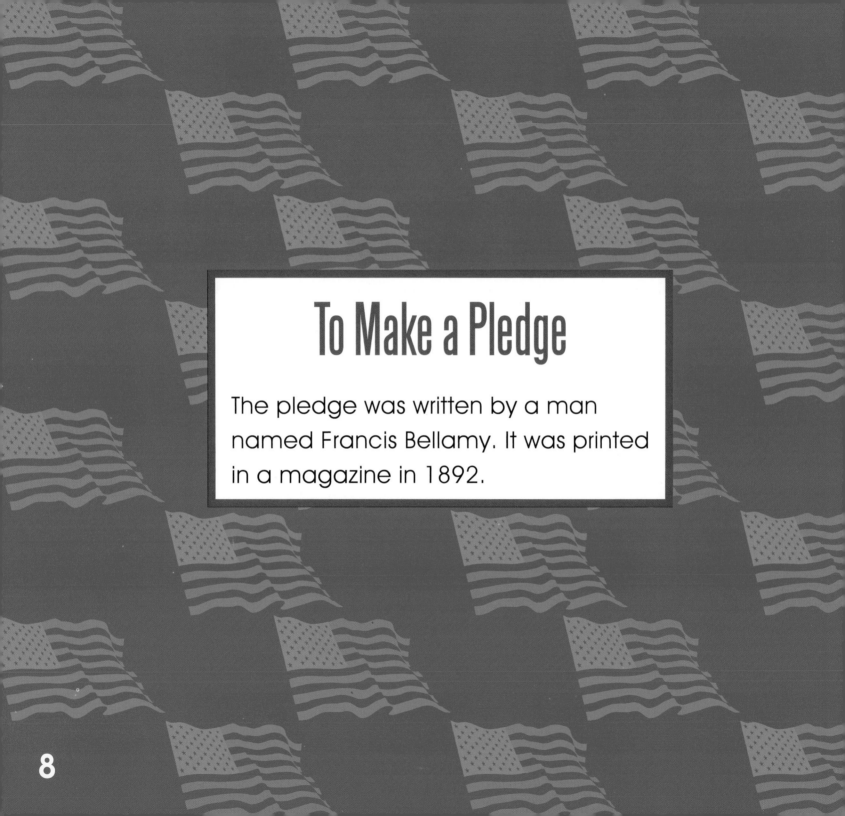

To Make a Pledge

The pledge was written by a man named Francis Bellamy. It was printed in a magazine in 1892.

9

The First Pledge

The Pledge of Allegiance was sent to schools across the country. Children said the pledge as part of a special event.

Facing the Flag

People face the flag to say the Pledge of Allegiance. They used to salute the flag with their right arm.

Changing Words

The words to the pledge were changed in 1923. The new words made the pledge only about the United States.

The Flag Code

The pledge became part of the flag code in 1942. The flag code is a set of rules about the American flag. A new rule told people to say the pledge with their right hand over their heart.

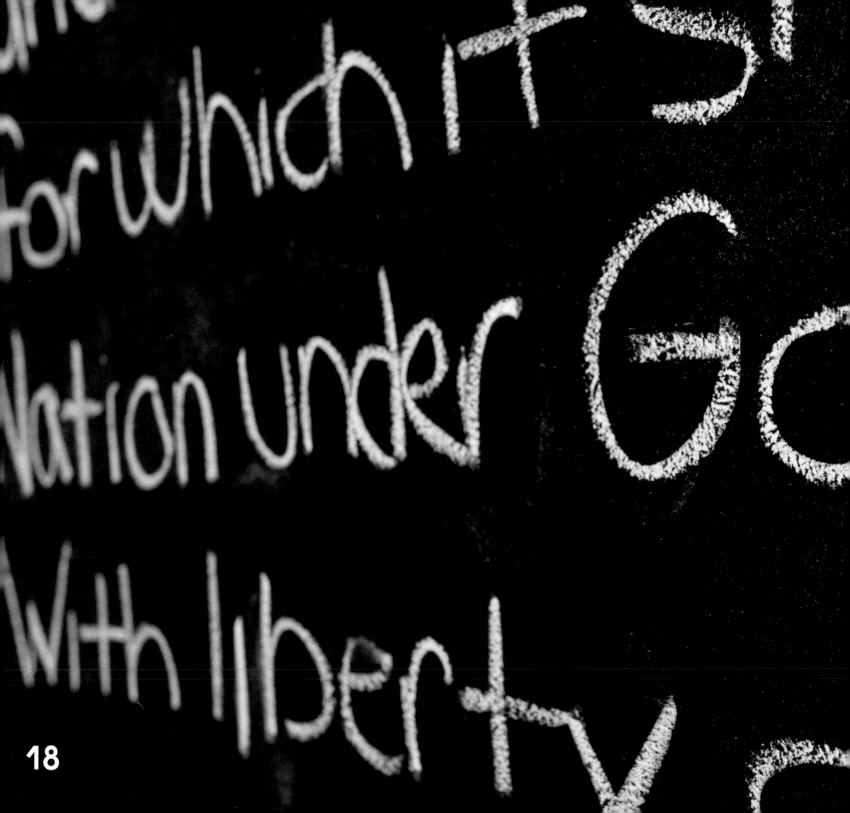

18

One More Change

Another change was made to the pledge in 1954. The words "under God" were added to the pledge. The pledge has not changed since.

The Pledge of Allegiance Today

Today, people can choose if they want to say the pledge or not. It is still said in many schools across the country. It is also said at the start of government meetings.

PLEDGE OF ALLEGIANCE FACTS

These pages provide detailed information that expands on the interesting facts found in the book. These pages are intended to be used by adults to help young readers round out their knowledge of each national symbol featured in the *American Icons* series.

Pages 4–5

What Is the Pledge of Allegiance? The Pledge of Allegiance was created as a show of patriotism. It was meant to coincide with the 400th anniversary of the arrival of Christopher Columbus in the New World. A national holiday was planned for October 1892 to mark the occasion, and the pledge was to be part of it.

Pages 6–7

A National Symbol With the Civil War ending just 27 years earlier, the Pledge of Allegiance quickly became a symbol of national unity. It also was recognized as a concise summary of the fundamental beliefs of freedom and justice upon which the United States was built. As such, the pledge soon came to be representative of the nation and its people.

Pages 8–9

To Make a Pledge The pledge was written in 1892 by Frances Bellamy, a Baptist minister from New York. It was published in a magazine called *The Youth's Companion*, without credit to the writer, in September of that year. The lack of credit sparked a controversy later when Bellamy and the magazine's editor, James B. Upham, both claimed to have written it. After an investigation, Bellamy was declared the author.

Pages 10–11

The First Pledge The Pledge of Allegiance was first spoken by schoolchildren across the United States in October 1892. As part of an official Columbus Day national celebration, the pledge was recited in unison as the American flag was raised to end the ceremonies. Schools quickly took to the pledge, and it soon became a daily fixture in many classrooms.

Pages 12–13

Facing the Flag The Pledge of Allegiance was meant to be spoken while facing the American flag. People were to stand up straight and hold their right arm out. The right hand was to be open, with the arm raised at an upward angle. This became known as the Bellamy Salute, for the author of the pledge.

Pages 14–15

Changing Words In 1923, the words of the pledge were changed for the first time. Bellamy originally wrote the pledge so that it could be used in any country. However, politicians were worried that new citizens could be saying the pledge while thinking of their former country's flag. Changing "my flag" to "the flag of the United States" made this clear. A year later, "of America" was added as well.

Pages 16–17

The Flag Code In 1942, the Pledge of Allegiance became an official part of the United States Flag Code. With World War II being fought in Europe, Americans began to be uncomfortable with the Bellamy Salute. They felt it was too similar to salutes used by the enemy Nazis and Fascists. When the flag code was passed, Congress changed the salute.

Pages 18–19

One More Change A final change was made to the Pledge of Allegiance in 1954. The words "under God" were added to the pledge. This was because the government of the time wanted to recognize the guidance of God in the country's affairs. President Dwight Eisenhower signed the change into law on June 14.

Pages 20–21

The Pledge of Allegiance Today The Pledge of Allegiance is still widely spoken across the country. However, people have a constitutional right to choose whether or not they recite the pledge. At least 45 states allow time for children to recite the pledge in school. Individual schools, teachers, and students each have the right to decide if this time will be used.

KEY WORDS

Research has shown that as much as 65 percent of all written material published in English is made up of 300 words. These 300 words cannot be taught using pictures or learned by sounding them out. They must be recognized by sight. This book contains 60 common sight words to help young readers improve their reading fluency and comprehension. This book also teaches young readers several important content words, such as nouns. These words are paired with pictures to aid in learning and improve understanding.

Page	Sight Words First Appearance
4	a, Americans, be, country, is, of, say, show, that, the, their, they, to, what
7	after, an, came, end, was
8	by, in, it, make, man, named
11	as, children, first, part, said, schools
12	face, people, right, used, with
15	about, changed, made, new, only, were, words
16	hand, over, set
19	another, has, more, not, one, under
20	also, at, can, if, many, or, still, want

Page	Content Words First Appearance
4	flag, Pledge of Allegiance, promise, United States
7	Civil War, symbol
8	Francis Bellamy, magazine
12	arm, salute
16	flag code, heart
20	government meetings

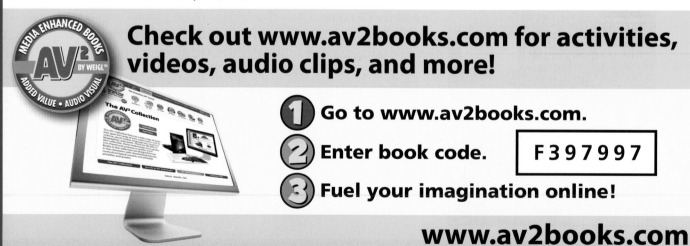

Check out www.av2books.com for activities, videos, audio clips, and more!

1 Go to www.av2books.com.

2 Enter book code. F397997

3 Fuel your imagination online!

www.av2books.com